IN APPRECIATION FOR BEING A PART OF

CSLA CONGRESS 94

Creative Direction
& Photo Selection
Karl Spreitz

Text
Cheryl Coull

Graphic Design
Karen Hodgson

Art Assistance
Lyn Quan

Front Cover
Brentwood Bay, Saanich Inlet..
Wayne Maloff photograph

Inside Front Cover
In memoriam: This stand near
Atluck Lake no longer exists.
Craig Hodgson photograph.

Inside Back Cover
Pacific storm off Wickaninnish,
west coast of Vancouver Island.
Mark Hobson photograph.

Published by
Beautiful British Columbia,
a Division of Jim Pattison
International Ltd.
John L. Thomson, President;
Tony Owen, Director of Publishing;
Bryan McGill, Editor.

To order copies of this book call
1-800-663-7611 in Canada or
(604) 384-5456 worldwide.
Fax: (604) 384-2812.

Beautiful British Columbia,
929 Ellery Streeet,
Victoria, B.C.,
V9A 7B4.

Printed and bound in Hong Kong
by NCP Industries Ltd.

Canadian Cataloguing in Publication Data

Main entry under title:
Vancouver Island--in search of the dream

ISBN 0-920431-09-7 (case)

1. Vancouver Island (B.C.). I. Beautiful
British Columbia Magazine (Firm)
FC3844.4.V35 1992   971.1'2   C92-091291-5
F1089.V3V35   1992

VANCOUVER ISLAND

In Search of the Dream

BEAUTIFUL BRITISH COLUMBIA

A Regional Portrait

Maple leaves return to the moss and fern-coated forest floor.

Vancouver Island, named and mapped

200 years ago, is still inviting a new way

of seeing things.

Its Restless Form

Trillium, a protected forest flower.

On the very north tip, the end only for some, is the beginning. The Transformer touched down on wind-swept shores, as Raven. And here, on this white wattle of sand, where the west coast is also the east, and the Inside is Out, where no humans lived then, or for that matter now, he made some. People. Then flew on – *kwaak kwaak* – strutting and waddling over the world that was an island, disappearing into the mists and fogs and rains of time, then reappearing. To set things right if they'd gone wrong. Turning landforms, seaforms, otherforms into peopleforms, and vice versa if they became forgetful, or ungrateful of their genesis. Back and forth. This is one story about how this island came to be. It didn't happen all at once. And it isn't finished.

Another story about how Vancouver Island came to be says millions of years ago, when time moved more slowly, there was sea and land, like now. Sometimes the sea covered the land, sometimes, it didn't. Finally, the earth itself became restless, heaving, convulsing, spitting and splashing red hot rock from the depths, throwing mountains walls up into the sky. Then everything cooled. Then, froze.

Temperate rain forest.

As much as this place is fragile, it is powerful.

As much as it can be changed by people,

it changes them.

An ecosystem like no other on earth.

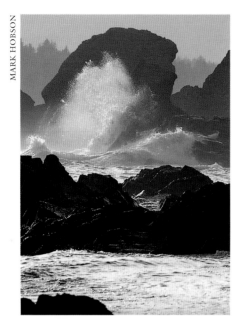

Surf-battered Bunsby Islands, off the north coast of Vancouver Island.

To understand this island is to understand the sea around it. The Pacific, its moods, its colours, are reflected in the sky, in the coastline, in the people.

The Pacific Ocean, Pacific Rim National Park.

A limestone peak near Sutton Pass, west of Port Alberni.

At the summit of Mariner Mountain, Strathcona Provincial Park.

ADRIAN DORST

In the Pinder Range, northern Vancouver Island.

CRAIG HODGSON

MARK HOBSON

Glaciers, a mile deep, pressed heavily on the new ranges – the Vancouver Island Mountains, the Coast Mountains to the east, and the Olympic Mountains to the south – before slipping into the dry troughs that lay in between them. The straits: now called Georgia and Juan de Fuca. The glaciers carved out new ledges, valleys, and lowlands, leaving steamy islets of earth behind. Then the sea rose again, drowning the lower peaks, which became sea-mounts – like Union, Explorer, and Heck – still attached to the continent by shelves and valleys of land underwater. The higher mountains became, altogether, this great island; their slopes became its shores. Their valleys are now fjords, inlets, and bays.

Forests grew up and made a home for Vancouver Island marmots, a species found in no other place; also black-tailed deer, Roosevelt elk, cougars, wolves, bears. Five species of salmon swam in the rivers and streams. And, along these western shores of the Pacific Ocean, birds, seals, sea lions, and sea otters flourished.

But this story too, still isn't finished.

Only when looking at a map of Vancouver Island is there a clear, unchanging circumscription of things. The main body is grey whale in shape. The highest peaks of the Vancouver Island ranges are right in the centre, like a hump, or saddle. This southwestern offspring of British Columbia measures 32,261 square kilometres. The distance, northwest to southeast, from Cape Scott to Victoria, is 451 kilometres. Even the convolutions of shoreline have been estimated: 3,440 kilometres on Vancouver Island and 2,480 kilometres more, on 2,000 encircling islets and islands, including the idyllic Gulf Islands archipelago.

Maps are useful, but they are illusions. This is the one thing that becomes clearer to all who have ever entered the straits with their eyes open. The size and shape of Vancouver Island, even its precise location, are up to the waves, tides, wind, rain, and fog. You can never truly be sure, because inlets become straits become peninsulas become islands become whales. Peaks could be fins. Ripples. Otters. Kelp beds. Seals. Dark things bobbing in the grey-green sea, appearing and disappearing, may be driftwood, or Raven.

Vancouver Island's black-tailed deer are plentiful under cover of the forest canopy.

Only three percent of the island's population lives in the vast northern half, still a frontier of loggers, miners, and fishermen.

Mook Peak, and the glowing lights of Woss,
a small logging community on northern Vancouver Island.

Totem erected 1929 at Friendly Cove.

ADRIAN DORST

The First People

From the time when potlatches were given openly, as they are again now: A chief from the north coast, or maybe, the west or southeast coast of the island thought it prudent to show his generosity to other chiefs. Wind and tides helped bring his canoe to the pebbled shores of a distant inlet. "To invite you to my potlatch", he said, suggesting a circle with his hand, "I have paddled all the way around the world."

Island-world. Spirit-world. Earth-world. There are those who say the First Peoples' understanding of it rivalled that of the ancient Greeks. That they had a way of seeing it and speaking about it that could only come from always having been here. They have no memory of fleeing any other kingdom – not Asia as is some times posited, by a land bridge over the Bering Sea. A bridge that vanished 10,000 years ago. These are people of the sea, as comfortable on its waves and beaches as sea froth: a bridge wouldn't have been necessary.

And yet, though they would name every headland, every cave and stream, there was no name for the whole of it. Their northern counter-parts, the Haida – The People – called their triangular archipelago *Haida-Gwaii* – Land of the People. The occupants of this much larger *gwaii* did not call it Vancouver *Gwaii*, or any such thing.

They did not have one name for the island, or for themselves. They were, and still are, three very distinct islands of people, differing vastly in language, and even subtly, in looks. Backs to the land, faces to the sea: to the north and northeast, the Kwakiutl. Carvers. They transformed

Performance of the Kwakiutl "Bumble Bee" dance, at the Lekwammon Longhouse in Esquimalt.

CHRIS CHEADLE

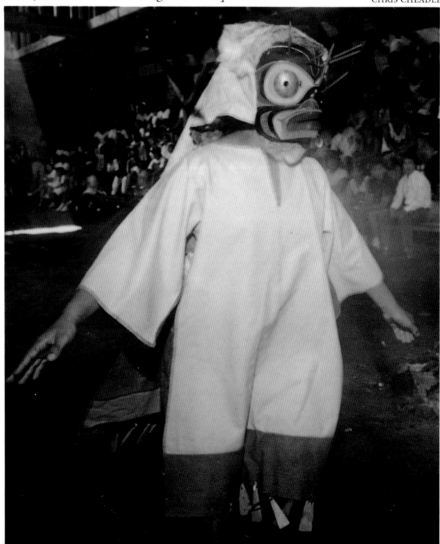

pieces of cedar into Bear, Eagle, Whale, Raven. Magicians, ribald and emulous, they used real magic sometimes, and often for fun, tricks – smoke and mirrors – to entertain their neighbours. Those looking west: the Nuu-chah-nulth, deep-voiced singers, peopling that longest wave-wind-storm-thrashed coast in inestimable numbers. Enduring, persisting, singing ancient whaling songs and dancing ancient dances, in five great ocean sounds full of inlets – now Quatsino, Kyuquot, Nootka, Clayoquot, Barkley – slicing the west edge of the island into five nearly equal parts. To the south and east, backs to the land, and facing the land too in a way, the Coast Salish people, whose seas are the gentler and sun-drenched straits. Some say the Coast Salish are gentler too, more poetic, in nature.

George Hunt Jr., Kwakiutl artist.

Rain falling on the far shores of Sproat Lake.

Nitinat Lake at the edge of the west coast.

Rain-forest totem.

On Vancouver Island, within the three Islands of People, there were more islands still: villages of hundreds and thousands of people, and within those, clans, and families; the more land in between them, the more likely a feather or two of difference in the brown-green of eyes, in ways of saying things, and stories.

And in privileges. Who can be Thunderbird, who can be Wolf, who can be waves can be Kingfisher. Whoever received the secrets, knows the song and wears the crest.

The Ahousat people of Clayoquot Sound could perform the Whale Ceremony, as could the people who lived at Neah Bay to the south, across Juan de Fuca Strait. With the ceremony, came *Osemitch*, purification, and the power of transformation. Chief becomes whale becomes whale hunter: swimming between islands to be strong, like *Ma'ak*, grey whale. Rubbing skin with sharp hemlock branches, as protection against drowning. Going without sleep, as *Ma'ak* would, for days or weeks till he surrendered. Praying, for *Ma'ak* to come willingly this time, and for his return.

This was a time when more supernatural things happened.

On rock bluffs facing the sea, washed or submerged by the tides – petroglyphs – an ancient record of island creatures mythical and real.

Petroglyph Park, near Nanaimo.

Orca, or killer whales, on the move.

13

Black bear.

G. PATRICK GREEN

Abundance allowed the First Peoples time to celebrate their relationship with the creatures in the world around them.

Black-tailed deer.

About 30 pods of killer whales live year-round off Vancouver Island.

Whaling, a Coal Harbour wood carving.

Moon-snail shell.

Tides of Change

Seas rose then fell. Ice came then went. People became. Time was marked by hundreds and thousands of generations of story-tellers, and by the tides that left circles around rocks and sunken canoes. The odd guest found a way in through the obscuring fog, but – until about eight generations ago – the tides of change lapped gently and slowly against the island's many shores.

Who the earliest visitors were is hard to measure by the features that distinguish them or the changes they wrought, for just as they would have altered the island, they too were altered by it. In Ahousat, people speak of a fair-skinned race they call *Ya-ae*, supernatural beings who passed the whaling ceremonies to their former neighbours, the Oo-tsus-aht, 500 years ago. The Oo-tsus-aht have since, themselves dissolved, no more than a generation ago, but they were said to be fair people, and some of them had grey eyes.

A race for the (Spanish) King's trophy.

Celebrating the bicentennial of Sooke's discovery by the Spanish.

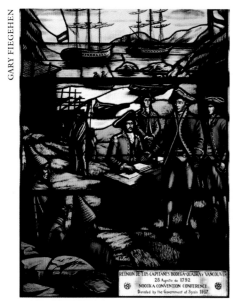

Stained-glass church window, Friendly Cove.

Time, moving forward.

Other calling cards left by the tides of change: A Japanese sword. A renowned anthropologist, Marius Barbeau, detects the "flavour" of Buddhist temple chanting in northwest coast tribal music. And in China, a scholar stumbles across the very detailed accounts of a Buddhist monk named Huei Shan, who returned home from wanderings in the *east* in 499 A.D.

1592 Juan de Fuca, working for Spain, claims to have sailed round Cape Flattery, at the entrance to the strait that now bears his name, expecting to come out on Hudson's Bay. His vision enhanced by his hopes, de Fuca notes here an inlet which might lead to the heart of the continent.

1774 Another Juan, Perez, seeking to expand the kingdom of Spain, waits off the entrance to Nootka Sound: the weather keeps him from landing.

1777 Britain's great navigator, Captain Cook, passes Cape Flattery, and records: "It is in this very latitude where we now are, that geographers have placed the pretended Straits of Juan de Fuca. But we saw nothing, nor is there the slightest probability that any such ever existed."

1778 Cook, still looking for de Fuca's "mythical" strait, sails north into a small inlet (unaware it's an island). There are people on shore.

(Meantime, the people on shore debate the nature of the thing floating in their bay. Maquinna, the chief, sees the deity *Qua-utz*, who disappeared across the sea, and was to return in a copper boat rowed by young men. His companion, Nanaimis, thinks it's a floating island carried on the back of *Huyitliik*, the lightning snake. Someone proposes an enchanted salmon. They canoe out to establish a relationship with it. Hailing "Nootka." Cook records this as their name, and gives it to everyone he meets up and down the coast. Two hundred years later, people who live in these inlets still laugh. Their relatives at this place, really called *Yuquot*, they say, were advising the enchanted salmon to circle round, so it wouldn't be injured on the hidden rocks.)

British things are exchanged for thick dark animal pelts – sea otter and

beaver – including, in a frenzy of giving, one the chief wore. Cook, pleased, raises his flag, claiming this land and all its fine pelts for his king.

1785 Nootka, international trading centre. Many vessels come and go. In China, sea otter furs are all the rage.

1787 Charles Barkley sees a large body of water which looks like it could be the one de Fuca described. He names it the Strait of Juan de Fuca.

1788 James Meares arrives at Nootka via the Orient carrying plans to build a schooner, Chinese labourers, and Maquinna's brother Comekela, the Travelled One, who had sailed off on another trading vessel and was abandoned in China.

1789 Don Estevan Martinez arrives at Nootka and declares it the dominion of the King of Spain.

The British express outrage. Two great world powers, and their allies, move to the brink of war over a misty islet.

1790 The Nootka Convention declares the willingness of both parties to negotiate.

ROLF BETTNER

Victoria's Market Square offers everything a traveller could want.

1792 Captain George Vancouver rounds Cape Flattery en route to "Nootka", where he will discuss the terms of the Nootka Convention with Juan Francisco de la Bodega y Quadra in a civilized manner. He detours into the Strait Juan de Fuca. As he sails northwest behind the Spaniards, giving British names to islands and inlets, he determines he has not found the Northwest Passage; what he is naming are the straits around a very large island. This he names too: *Quadra's and Vancouver's Island.* Eventually, "Quadra's" is dropped.

1795 Britain and Spain abandon Nootka and its chief, but the fierce trade for sea otter pelts continues.

1834 American whaling ships are active off the coast, harvesting the slow-swimming humpback whales, grey whales, blue whales, minke whales.

1842 Hudson's Bay Company factor James Douglas selects Vancouver Island's southern tip as the "perfect Eden" for the island's first non-native settlement, really the second after Nootka, where both Europeans and Chinese had lived. Douglas calls it Fort Camousun, for the people who live there, but later renames it to honour his queen, Victoria. Population 50, settlement not encouraged.

1849 Vancouver Island is declared a British colony.

1858 Victoria wakes up, port of entry and supply centre for thousands of gold rushers en route to the mainland. British people settle here. Also Chinese, Japanese, Germans, Swedes, Norwegians, Dutch, Czechs, Hungarians, Americans. It's difficult to say who didn't come.

1866 The British colony of Vancouver Island and the adjacent mainland colony form a united British Columbia.

1868 The local whaling industry is launched in Saanich Inlet, near Victoria. Passengers on coastal steamers are dining on a wonderful new delicacy, "sea beef."

1871 New colony joins new country, Canada. A railway linking island to continent has been promised, but never arrives. In the meantime, however, a thousand ships a year connect Victoria to every major port in world, and the pelagic sealing industry, employing thousands on more than 100 schooners helps establish Victoria as a major port of its day. The estimated five million fur seals in the North Pacific will be decimated within the next three decades.

Bob Lawrence, volunteer steam train conductor, B.C. Forest Museum.

PAUL FLETCHER

JEFF BARBER/INFOCUS

Craigflower Manor built in 1856, near Victoria.

Emily Carr's family home, built in 1863, on Victoria's Government Street.

JEFF BARBER/INFOCUS

The knobby peninsula at the south tip was chosen

the "perfect Eden" for Vancouver Island's first

non-native settlement.

Craigflower Manor is now a national historical site.

Sea anemones, starfish, sea urchin.

North end of Long Beach.

The Sea and Tides

The story, and stories, of Vancouver Island return again and again to the sea. Stories of floods and riptides and shipwrecks and sea monsters. Stories of harpooned whales being found with tiny legs in place of their fins, further suggesting that whales, like stories, prefer the sea. Stories with no plot at all, of days spent combing the beach for whatever is there.

The Nuu-chah-nulth tell how Thunderbird, crying for his wife *Qolus* gone to live among human-forms, nearly drowned earth completely. Another story says The Flood was in 1964. And it wasn't just an ordinary flood either. It was a tidal wave, a *sunami*, with all the power of a quaking earth and the sun-moon-tides behind it. Over a period of 24 hours it hit Vancouver Island's west coast again and again, gaining strength as it funnelled up inlets. Its message hit hardest in the most inland city of all. Port Alberni, at that time in its heyday, still expanding up into the Beaufort Mountains from its docks and mills at the head of the island's longest inlet. A full 40 kilometres from the open coast. The seas rose nearly three metres above high water, measured by the marks left on houses: the recorder had gone right off the scale. People looked out their windows and saw their cars floating by.

After the waters receded, at a time when people were no longer in the habit of investing "natural" events with any larger meaning at all, there was just a hint of awe in their voices. *The Flood came to Us.* On the average, *sunamis* happen about once a year. Usually amounting to only a few centimetres, there's not much to say. Floods don't happen every day.

Tides, on the other hand, do. The sea rises, it falls. In out, up down, ebb flow, twice a day. The Saxons took their word for time, and hence ours, from the word tide. But on Vancouver Island, one of the most inleted and islanded coasts on earth, tide takes its own time, *island* time, not the same time every day, or everywhere.

Glaucous-winged gull and chicks.

Wickaninnish Centre, Long Beach, Pacific Rim National Park.

There are magic places,

linked more easily by water

than by roads.

Clayoquot Sound, Long Beach in the foreground.

The tufted puffin is occasionally glimpsed.

THOMAS KITCHIN

From old growth springs new growth.

GARTH LENZ

The island's dominant hemlocks are commonly used for producing pulp.

Vancouver Islanders continue to live within the concentric circles of tide-time. Especially clam diggers, mussel gatherers, back-to-the-landers, and natives who haven't lost their taste for a salty tale and slippery sea-things like chiton and sea urchin and sea cucumber. People who still say "Dinner is when the tide goes out." Out in the straits, shippers, fishermen trolling or trailing gill nets, and tugboaters hitched to island-sized log booms, all fluctuate with the tide's time. Wondering, whoever said predictable as the tides. It's more like come hell or high water. Predictable maybe, if wind and fog were, too.

Riptides are places where the sea meets itself coming and going, or where a strong current going one way meets wind going the other, responding with confusion and violence. An intense example of this is in the narrow channels round "back" of the island. Where persistent tides travelling from Cape Scott south between islets meet themselves coming north through the Gulf Islands in Juan de Fuca and Georgia straits. There are many places in Discovery Pass, most infamously Seymour Narrows, where currents run up to 10 knots, that's about 19 kilometres per hour.

Perilous tides giving life to the island. In one litre of this churning amniotic fluid, someone counted 60 million microscopic plants and animals of some 3,000 varieties. Plankton, feeding herring, feeding five species of salmon, halibut, cod, feeding seals, feeding whales, feeding people. Thousands of people each year arrive in Campbell River, overlooking Discovery Pass, for the express purpose of hooking big salmon.

On the "outside", along the west coast, active tidal waters turn rock crevices and soft sandstone shelves, such as those at Botanical Beach, 95 kilometres northwest of Victoria, into tide pools: cauldrons of life supporting exotic profusions of intertidal sea life. Sea palms, sea-robins that change their colour to match the rocks, encrusted coralline algae. Sea anemones of unearthly colours, starfish, mussels.

Surf and rocks, Pacific Rim National Park.

This edible fungus is called "chicken of the woods."

MARK HOBSON

Beyond the surf, beneath the canopy of trees, there is safety.

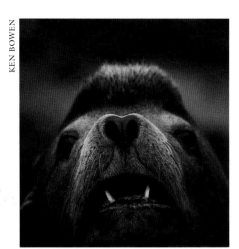

Steller's sea lion.

On this raggedy edge,
where forces are enough to
alter the shape of continents,
amazing things cling and
flourish. Some are rock hard,
others delicate and soft.

*Seaweed on the most wave-battered shores
is as thick and varied as forest plants.*

GRAHAM OSBORNE

Cormorants on the rocks.

Pacific Rim National Park.

Tides of life, reversing, becoming tides of death. Red tides, caused by tiny algae that thrive in the months with no "R", when there is sunlight, and the water is, relatively, warm. Staining water the colour of blood. There is no harm done to the filter-feeding shellfish – mussels, oysters, clams – that ingest them, but any human who eats the tainted shellfish is dining on one of the most toxic natural poisons on earth. First, tingling, then numbness, muscular paralysis, and finally death by asphyxiation.

Tides joining forces with that trickster, fog. Transforming rocks into hidden dangers. Turning open passages into unavoidable bluffs. Tides combining with wind blowing from the southeast at 100 kilometres an hour, and faster in gusts – to turn Vancouver Island's southwest coast into the "Graveyard of the Pacific".

"Forty wrecks for every mile", they say, between Port Renfrew and Barkley Sound, where there is no safe inlet for any ship in any weather, though it was winter that took most of them. No one really knows how many or when. But as early as 1786, two British ships engaged in the sea otter trade were lost, along with their crews. In the two centuries since, some sailors have made it safely to shore clinging to rope or life raft, or by being pulled into canoes by "search and rescue teams" comprised of natives. Others haven't.

In 1906, perhaps the worst disaster of all. An American Steamer, the *Valencia*, ground onto the rocks at Pachena Point. Would-be rescuers watched helplessly as 126 of 164 passengers and crew perished in the sea. In response, the following year, construction began on a life-saving trail to cut 70 kilometres through the confusion, hunger, and cold that awaited survivors on shore. Cabins along the way were stocked with medical supplies, food, matches, dry firewood, even telephones and instructions in several languages on how to use them.

Canada geese fly by Comox Glacier.

Wolfe Lake in the Nimpkish Valley.

Nurse log for new trees in the Walbran Valley.

Skunk cabbage.

Today 1,000 beacons, lighthouses, foghorns, markers and buoys line coastal corridors like streetlights. Radar, long-range navigational aids, and rescue technology have all helped. The most recent shipwreck along the Graveyard was March 14, 1972 when the *Vanlene*, an 8,000-tonne freighter carrying cars to Vancouver from Japan hit the rocks off Austin Island. This time, the crew, and even some of the cars were air-lifted to safety.

That life-saving trail is now the West Coast Trail. Hikers come from all over the world to enjoy, and "endure", a week of island meeting sea. And there is always a story to tell: seven days of sun, or seven of rain and blisters, killer whales, grey whales, eagles. Connections made to others, to self, to this island.

The trail is part of the vast and wonderful entity called Pacific Rim National Park, encompassing more than 500 square kilometres of quintessential coast. It incorporates the 100 and more islands of Barkley Sound's magical Broken Group: crescent-shaped beaches, forests, native middens, fishermans' cabins, California and Steller's sea lions, safe landings for kayakers, canoeists, sailors, powerboaters.

And it takes in Long Beach with its seemingly miraculous expanses of sand and driftwood between the villages of Tofino and Ucluelet, 41 kilometres apart. For many, even those who have never faced the open Pacific before, there is an instant sense of relief upon seeing the capped breakers spuming and rolling up onto shore. In hearing them thunder, then sigh in retreat, and in feeling the mist of salty sea on their faces. A sense of relief, joined with return. Nearly a million people a year make this pilgrimage.

In early spring, they scan the blue-green waves for the telltale spume of grey whales on their way from breeding waters in Mexico to feeding grounds in the Bering Sea. Thousands and thousands will pass by. In summer months, people scuff along in the sand, looking for Japanese glass floats, poking mounds of seaweed with driftwood sticks. Adjusting their own internal and external rhythms to those of the sea. In fall, more come, to watch over the whales; moving south again. Here, the tenor of stories is more of mutual vulnerability: there is much more a sense of the need to protect the sea, than a need to be protected from it.

Opposite: Trees support moss, ferns.

The Way Inland

Shipwrecked sailors and west-coast hikers know how hard it can be to get to some place dry. Walls of blinding rain offer no handholds, rocks and cliffs roofed by wind-bent salal may have no way through. A headland eventually cuts in, but the coast is a maze, and the odds favour another nowhere-to-go.

If the outside was tense, the inside can be creepy to the uninitiated. Creepy from sucking sounds underfoot – slugs, fungi, mud-covered roots, decomposing mushrooms, decomposing trees, dripping ferns, skunk cabbage.

The Japanese current acts like a blanket, warm – but that's relative – and wet. Absolutely. Carrying air from the tropics, it collides with the island's outer coast. The wettest weather station in North America is at Henderson Lake, near Ucluelet, at the northeast corner of Barkley Sound, where a yearly average of 6,550 millimetres (22 feet) of water pours from the sky. One day in December, 1926 more than 415 millimetres came down. Knee high on a short man if he stood there all day.

On the west coast alone, 81 rivers, plus creeks and spontaneous rivulets drain the excess. Water falls from rocky edges to ledges to cliffs onto beaches. Della Falls, in Strathcona Provincial Park above Great Central Lake, is Canada's highest, and, at 440 metres, sixth highest on this planet. In one or two places, water percolates up from the island's warm bowels. At Hot Springs Cove it's almost too hot to touch till after it has made its miraculous way through forest, over ledge, and into three healing pools washed by the sea.

Experiment Bight, Cape Scott Provincial Park.

The powdery dudleya is found on rocky bluffs by the sea.

Sea lions in the surf near Bamfield.

KARL SPREITZ

*Lone Cone Mountain on Meares Island, above
and opposite, viewed from sea and land.*

Fog is trickster, wind its companion, transforming

the island from one moment to the next.

Tobogganing at Mount Washington.

Taps to the sea always on, and still there are 2,000 lakes on Vancouver Island. Some nearly oceans themselves in size and nature: Great Central, Campbell, Kennedy, Sproat, Nimpkish, Cowichan, Buttle, each 15 to 40 kilometres of steel-grey waters surrounded by steep-sided shores and haunted by quick-tempered winds. Nitinat Lake, on the west coast, is actually connected to the Pacific Ocean by Nitinat Narrows. Halfway to being an inlet, this 24-kilometre lake smells like the sea and has tides, constant winds, "confused sea" conditions, and a pioneering population of jellyfish, sea anemones, and starfish.

Parts of this island resemble a sponge. A temperate rain-forest sponge. An ecosystem – trees, soil, wildlife, fish, waterways – of global significance. There are few places like it on earth. From its watersheds have risen the world's tallest, widest, oldest trees.

Giant among giants, the red cedars, and giant among them, in Pacific Rim National Park, a tree 2,100 years old. Old when Christ was young. It's taller than a 20-storey building, and

four people fingertip to fingertip cannot reach around it. The island's prevailing trees are Douglas fir and Sitka spruce, between 300 and 800 years old, rising, often, 90 metres high. Canada's tallest Douglas fir stands on a tiny Nimpkish Valley island. A youth at 400, it's 90 metres tall and still growing. The oldest known Douglas fir, near Port Renfrew, is 900, but, with a broken top, it's now just 73 metres high. The biggest Sitka spruce are in the Carmanah Valley, southwest on the island. Here, among a relatively small stand of hundreds averaging 85 metres tall, is what may be the largest Sitka spruce in the world, rising yet another 10 metres above the creek bank.

Such enumerations sound impressive, but what was once blanketing most of Vancouver Island has been reduced to patches: thick-barked survivors of an ice age, fires, and logging that occurred at a rate of 500 square kilometres a year. Most of the island's old-growth forest has either been logged, or until recent changes in government policy, was slated for the chain saw. Only about five percent of this forest that will take several of our lifetimes to grow back, yet remains, some of it preserved, in Pacific Rim National Park, and in provincial parks like Strathcona, Schoen Lake, Cape Scott, Macmillan (Cathedral Grove), and Carmanah.

Opposite: Cross-country ski trails at Mount Washington.

Fog plays with lake contours.

NEIL FALLAS

A bout going inland, scrambling from the outside to places in, the Old Storytellers hush. To them, the forest groves are cathedrals. And only deep inside are there long shafts of light revealing the dry places.

The forest keeps the rains from washing everything away. It is a buffer between the sea and the "sea of mountains" – the island's chaos of peaks that appears from a distance like petrified waves. They defy human patterns and anything much in the way of naming, beyond the "Vancouver Island", or sometimes, the "Insular" mountains. In the hump that is the geographical centre of the island there is, not one, but a triad of sacred peaks: Mount Golden Hinde at 2,200 metres, the highest. Elkhorn just northwest sits at 2,195 metres, and Albert Edward, just east, 2,081 metres.

Something about this unfrequented innermost place – glaciers, wildflower meadows, the first tricklings of island watersheds – inspired the creation of B.C.'s first provincial park, Strathcona. It stretches 70 kilometres by 90 kilometres by 55 kilometres, from Herbert Inlet due north to Gold Lake, then diagonally, southeast, beyond Oshinaw Lake. A pyramid of mountains on a triangular base. Just within its eastern boundary is Forbidden Plateau, one of Canada's oldest ski areas, and just outside, Mount Washington, with peaks and meadows that invite skiing or hiking, with sea and mountain views all the way to the mainland. Somewhere, up here too, is Thunderbird's dry aerie. Tucked between seas, between rain and rain shadow, he sleeps, and just dreams of hunting whales.

No place is more than 40 kilometres from the sea. Water is everywhere. Dripping from the tips of ferns, flowing and raging in streams and rivers.

The forests are cathedrals.

CRAIG HODGSON

The long blue-green fingers of Sproat Lake, near Port Alberni, are ideal for boating, swimming, and fishing.

Entering Royal Roads Military College, near Victoria.

Ross Bay Cemetery.

Island of Utopias

Island stories are full of new-comers making this utopia their own. Many of them would, if they could, let it float freer and farther still from the worlds they have left behind.

Vancouver Island's first utopian was John Mackay, a British surgeon, who, in 1786, with garden seeds, a hoe and two goats, volunteered himself "the first settler on the coast". He took leave of his ship, the *Experiment*, and rowed for the most rugged shores on this earth. Today there are no visible reminders of this man who offered fresh vegetables and hot rolls to sailors visiting Nootka. And there's just barely more – one family now – to remind us of the village-kingdom called *Yuquot*, presided over by generations of chiefs named Maquinna. The Europeans, who had dined here on solid silver plates, dissolved their remote Pacific outpost after eight years spent founding a "new" world. And in that short time, a maelstrom of native depopu-lation by smallpox, tuberculosis, venereal disease, and disruption had already begun.

By 1897, when a small group of Danes landed at the island's sand-swept north tip with their utopian dreams, they had it all to themselves. As did the Norwegians who around the same time named their chosen community Quatsino, after the native people who had recently abandoned

Basking in the island's shimmering waters.

this world of inlets. Nearly a century later, Quatsino persists with 91 people and no overland connection whatsoever to the rest of the world. As for the Danes' cooperative attempt at Cape Scott, there's not so much as a dot on the map. But their legacy is a 15,700-hectare provincial wilderness park. A long day's hike to some of the most beautiful wilderness beaches on earth, the remains of one final dike, a few farm buildings, and a tombstone, are monuments left to wind and waves.

Craigdarroch Castle, Victoria.

Sun and shadows, Central Saanich near Victoria.

*L*ess strength of conviction, more desire to leave things pretty much as they are seems to be a recipe for survival-of-some-kind among island utopias. An English-Irish religious sect had already fled Malcom Island in Queen Charlotte Strait when some Finns, cramping the style of a Danish hermit, created their "Place of Harmony" here. Sointula, so named in 1901 by its leader-philosopher Matti Kurrika, would subsist on cooperation and the laws of nature. They were a lot of poets, and knew little of timber or clams. Sointula *is,* still. Peopled by descendants of those that stayed, finding their own quiet way to reconcile principles with island realities.

Clo'oose came to be in 1911: a real estate adventure along what is now the West Coast Trail. Overlooking the Graveyard of the Pacific. Views. A seaside hotel, wide streets. A long wharf and railway spur line. All empty promises. But the gentle British men, women and children who invested their lives' savings held a stiff upper lip to the sand-shifting swells and the persistent beating of Indian drums. Clo'oose wasn't "officially abandoned" until 1966.

Tides of dreamers. Black slaves travelled across the continent in search of "true" freedom, and found it, on Salt Spring Island. Michael the Archangel led Russian Doukhobors to Hilliers, near the centre of the island. Nearby at Coombs, Ensign Crego of the Salvation Army founded a community for poor English and Welsh. Their descendants still celebrate simple country living with bluegrass music festivals, the Coombs Country Opera, and by keeping goats on the sod roof of the Old Country Market.

Tiger lily.

Opposite: Stables north of Victoria.

Cowichan Station, southeast Vancouver Island.

The pastoral southeast coast attracts the genteel and artistic.

TERRY PATTERSON

Sailing the Strait of Georgia.

GORDON J. FISHER/IMAGE FINDERS

The Spaniards explored these waters in 1792.

In the pastoral Cowichan Valley: a "Sportsman's Paradise", and a "little bit of Olde England". Afternoon tea, cricket, rugby, and a tennis club second only to Wimbledon in the entire British Commonwealth were promised, and delivered.

Brother Twelve, the twelfth master in a brotherhood said to guide the evolution of the human race, gathered a community of wealthy followers near Nanaimo, and later, created a

"City of Refuge" on nearby Cortez and Valdez islands, a bastion against the coming Armageddon. But here the bastion became a prison, and the prophet's followers became his slaves, as Armageddon turned on utopia.

Sombrio Beach, southwest coast, just beyond Sooke and its gentle harbour. A contemporary utopian scene: there are dozens of places like this. Crudely called squatters, these dreamers make no claims that extend beyond what they can see in the fog, and their shanties, cabins of ingenious design set unevenly midst trees facing the shore. Cedar, plastic floats, styrofoam and jetsam. Stages of permanence. They take pride in being different, and find themselves in a community of people just like them. Two or three have flourishing gardens visible. Three barrel-bellied goats are rummaging between beached driftwood logs. Glaring at the strangers. Someone has been carving porpoises, leaving them in the sand wherever a form has taken shape; there's a trail of porpoises along the shore. Behind this strange village, wide and well-worn trails wind through a see-through strip of giant rain forest. And behind it, a new clearcut grows.

Opposite: Fishing the Gorge, Victoria.

Ucluelet, a west coast logging-fishing-tourist village.

T h e   T o w n s

Four hundred and fifty kilometres of "island highway" connect the unexpected and incongruous. Most of Vancouver Island's cities, towns, and villages are along this long east-coast road most of the others are linked to it, either by logging roads or paved arteries that flow from the west, between island mountains. The west coast is too intangible for a road of its own.

The "island community", with a small-city's population of 574,000, is to some degree an invention of the highway. It's a long but possible day's drive from the first town, Port Hardy on the wild northeast coast, to Victoria, in the rain shadow at the south tip. New stretches of blacktop, bridges, and passing lanes have subdued the adventure of ferries, potholes, and oncoming logging trucks, but this is no freeway by any means. The old character of the island towns is still plain to see. And logging roads that end up in misty little villages are far from extinction.

KARL SPREITZ

Port Alberni's Harbour Quay.

JANICE CHEADLE

There is no solid line separating landforms and seaforms from the company of humanforms.

Hanging around the dock.

PAUL BAILEY

The sea is the focus of people-oriented development in Nanaimo.

Deep Bay lies on island's east coast, south of Courtenay.

From north to south – and west to east on the arteries – there is a tendency for two lanes to become four. Mysterious skies lift to become blue. Old rain forest, moonscapes of logged valleys, then second-growth forest open to the Strait of Georgia, glimpses of snowy Coast Mountains, islands and ferry docks, hotels and restaurants with recurring names: Sea Breezes, Sea Views, Bay Views. Pretty spots: Oyster Bay, Union Bay, Fanny Bay. In the towns along the way, there is a gradual building up of intensity, with the final burst just beyond the Malahat Mountains where half of the island population jostles for views from the gentle promontories and peninsulas of the capital region.

A few were, and still are, single industry towns. Whaling towns, fishing towns, logging towns, sawmill and pulp-mill towns, mining towns. Most, though, are fishing-logging-milling-mining towns. And in the past two decades, recognizing the need to grow, *i.e.* survive, beyond resource extraction, they have added tourism to their resumés. A renewable resource. Island towns that depended on and took pride in chopping down the biggest trees and hooking the biggest fish share a particular affinity for the Tallest, Widest, Longest, and Most Outrageous when it comes to advertising their attributes.

In Port Hardy, a carrot marks Mile Zero of *their* north island highway, the one that leads north from here yet, along the Inside Passage to Prince Rupert on the mainland, via BC Ferries' Queen of the North. Shimmering motorhomes are plugged into wild-wooded campsites; hotels and pubs are filled to the brim with loggers, miners, mud-caked hikers off the trail from Cape Scott, and sports fishermen who have been lured by tales of the big chinook salmon. Port McNeill, an instant logging town on a logged-off hillside where every house has a view, boasts the World's Largest Burl, 20 tonnes, taken from a 351-year-old spruce tree.

Such are the exaggerations of already existing extremes. On the road to Port Alice, in the middle of a forest of stumps: "the lushest greens on earth". The Seven Hills Golf and Country Club. Alert Bay, a half-native, half non-native village on tiny Cormorant Island claims the World's Tallest Totem Pole, 53 metres; more taxis per kilometre of road than any city in the world; an important native cultural centre, and a 110-year-old Anglican church.

Opposite: This island is still home to people who live and travel by the tide's time.

Near Crofton: farms, forest, and Gulf Islands.

Travellers have come here, to the edge of the world, and never left. Their reasons for staying are quietly respected.

Here is an industrial tourism that goes well beyond the hard-hatted horizons of mill tours. The arching jawbones of a blue whale mark Coal Harbour, facing west onto Holberg Inlet, in 1967 the island's last whaling station to close. A few kilometres southeast, Telegraph Cove, a former sawmill town of 22, propped enchantingly above Johnstone Strait on boardwalks, is the launching point for ecologically minded charters. Slipping out into the calm between misty islets, the world's largest cruise ships and log barges, small vessels go in search of totems, eagles, sea lions, and the families of killer whales that gather every summer at the gravelly mouth of the Tsitika River in Robson Bight to rub barnacles off their bellies.

Farther south, Chemainus, "The Little Town that Did". In the early 1980s when the 120-year-old sawmill closed up, a visionary member of the Chamber of Commerce "revitalized" the economy with a scheme that culminated in 30 larger-even-than-life murals: steam donkeys, steel cables, loggers straight-faced and glaring, real people from Chemainus's own history book, recreated on the exterior surfaces of the community's biggest buildings. Over 300,000 tourists a year became the new industry. Then a new sawmill opened, and *vi-o-la*, a town with two industries.

Meanwhile, two towns, one claim. Port Alberni, at the end of a 40-kilometre inlet, and Campbell River, at the end of a 180-metre pier built for the pure satisfaction of saltwater fishing: both the "Salmon Capital of the World".

Nanaimo. With six deep-sea docks, a major BC Ferry terminal, freighters, ferries, trollers and gillnetters, tug boats, sailboats, seaplanes and sea-walks, it's still the "The Bathtub Capital of the World." In its Annual Bathtub Festival, 200 motorized tubs race 54 kilometres across the Strait of Georgia's choppy waters to Vancouver. On it goes. Duncan, "City of Totems," home of the Cowichan people, B.C.'s largest native band, their expansive native cultural centre and "working" village. Also an ecomuseum – a museum without walls, the only one of its type in Canada – centred around the forest industry. *And* the World's Largest Hockey Stick. In a climate where just *ice* is considered extreme.

Opposite: A view of Mount Prevost from across the Cowichan Valley.

Many island towns
are just discovering their
own beauty and history;
turning a protective eye
to the environment
around them.

"Prince of the logging camp," Campbell River wood carving.

Campbell River overlooks Johnstone Strait and Quadra Island.

TERRY PATTERSON

Campbell River's saltwater fishing pier.

Island Towns. Some are quietly aware their treasures need not be measured, or counted, or named. Visitors will come, drawn by something inside themselves. They return again and again to gentle east-coast villages like Parksville and Qualicum, where unusual expanses of sand meet an unusually warm sea.

And west coast places, too. Bamfield sits, rain washed and isolated much of the year, shored up on boardwalks over the south edge of Barkley Sound. A fishing village essentially, linked to the world by unpaved roads ruled by logging trucks, and the *Lady Rose*, a small passenger and cargo ship serving the sound from Port Alberni. There are times when the 211 people who live here are nearly overcome by the tides of people – sports fishermen, hikers, kayakers, and poets seeking sandy bays, headlands, light-houses, and waterfalls along the first day or two of the West Coast Trail. The hundred islands of the Broken Group. Sea lions, whales, eagles.

Northwest of here, Tofino, on the tip of Esowista Peninsula near the entrance to Clayoquot Sound, collects the runoff from Pacific Rim National Park. Happy campers looking for a coffee shop, bakery or an art gallery to sit out the rain, or to hear from the locals what's going on. Not so much bragging as expressing their deeply held concerns about the logging, and the oil tankers passing by their vulnerable shores. The environmentalist message is everywhere, and spreading. It's a symbiotic relationship: people changing the face of the land; and the land – sea, forests, mountains – changing the people.

Classic sailboats at Victoria's Inner Harbour.

In the Rain Shadow

About the time Rudyard Kipling said: "To realize Victoria you must take all that the eye admires most in Bournemouth, Torquay, the Isle of Wight, the Happy Valley at Hong Kong – the Doon, Sorrento, and Camps Bay; add reminiscences of the Thousand Islands and arrange the whole around the Bay of Naples, with some Himalayas for the background," Thunderbird flew the coop.

The ruckus of too many humanforms stirred him from his rain shadow aerie on Mount Newton now encircled by greater Victoria. He flapped his thunderous eagle-wings. And withdrew, to the rugged ranges of Knight Inlet, up the coast.

Half of Vancouver Island's population, 300,000 people, have amassed on the south end's idyllic little knob. This, the other of two ends, is the one most connected to the rest of the world. Connected, by way of comparison – as Kipling, and many others have eloquently done. By proximity – it is nearly surrounded by mainland. The Canadian Gulf Islands and the American San Juans are stepping stones across the straits, and island-sized ferries – some carrying 1,500 people, and nearly 400 cars at a time – are a highway themselves to Vancouver, or to Port Angeles, Anacortes, and Seattle on the U.S. side of the 49th parallel. A line that if continued straight, would lop off a most precious fifth of the island, from Ladysmith south.

Connected by familiarity. In climate, appearance, and temperament, Victoria and the Saanich Peninsula are intensely pleasing to people who are not *from* the rain forest. It reminds them of places they've dreamed, Laceland or Laputa, an " 'Eden'... dropped from the clouds into its present position," wrote James Douglas. There is rain in the shadow. But no more than one would expect. Less than three cups a year. It is beauty – broad-leaved garry oak, slender ochre-skinned arbutus – *sans* the beast. Its magic is performed, fairly, in sunshine, not fog. In all directions, sea shimmers. Islands shimmer. Mountains mighty and majestic – Baker and the Olympics – closer and bluer some days than others. But even on hazier days there's an apparent clarity, a relative certainty that what you are seeing is what exists.

Sentinels of time, Victoria's Royal British Columbia Museum.

Rogue wave washes Dallas Road, Victoria.

Downtown Victoria, Juan de Fuca Strait, and the Olympic Mountains.

Midst the museums, symphonies and gardens

of Victoria in the rain shadow, it is easy to forget

Raven, strutting about, somewhere.

*Turn-of-the-century ornamentation:
images of permanence and prosperity.*

*Victoria maintains its
tradition of architectural pride.*

Double-decker buses tour Victoria, the Garden City.

Pedal-powered cab in Victoria's Beacon Hill Park.

Windsurfers off Dallas Road.

Butchart Gardens near Victoria.

KARL SPREITZ

Cruise ships dock at Victoria's Ogden Point.

A gilded statue of Captain Vancouver surveys Victoria's Inner Harbour from a copper dome high on the Parliament Buildings, the seat of the province's government. A very respectable, cosmopolitan, sophisticated city below him. By all means, a *capital* capital for tourists. Pavement and cobblestone, the old Empress Hotel serving high tea since 1908. Museums, galleries, antique and book shops, arboretums, convention centre, condominiums, cafés. Elegant horse-drawn carriages, double-decker buses, exotic peddle-powered Kabuki Kabs. Cruise ships, airplanes, sailboats, and windsurfers.

A cultured, and cultivated city. From the hanging flower baskets on Government Street, to the gardens and seaward-sloping meads of Beacon Hill Park, to Government House, to Craigdarroch Castle. To the manicured yards and estates of James Bay, Oak Bay, the Uplands, and Cadboro Bay. To the pastoral perfection of the Saanich Peninsula, and Butchart Gardens' 52 hectares of flowers near Brentwood Bay. Right to the tidy seaside town of Sidney, which lies between the international airport reporting more hours of sunshine than almost anywhere in Canada, and, the BC Ferries terminal. From whence the ships always sail.

Except once in a very stormy while. When rogue winds can bring the sea over the long breakwater at Ogden Point, and the fog horns start moaning. When, as in bygone days, coffins being set

to rest in the old Quadra Street Cemetery had to be held down, or stood upon, the tide tables had risen so high.

The Raven does dwell midst the rain shadow's openness and light. There are treacherous, racing, riptides at Race Rocks, the most southerly aspect of Vancouver Island. There is fog – 292 hours once, without lifting.

Mist wafts over Saanich Peninsula.

The pastoral Saanich Peninsula.

*The ivy-clad Empress Hotel, watching over Victoria's bustling
Inner Harbour since 1908.*

Occasionally fog descends upon the Inner Harbour and Parliament Buildings.

B ut the inscrutable is typically sailed around, not into.

Like Victoria's Chinatown at the turn of the century. Its fog of incense and opium, and the incessant clacking of mah jong tiles and forecasts from the *Book of Changes*, were contained within Fan Tan Alley. D'Arcy Island, between Saanich Peninsula and the mainland, from 1884-1925, a leper colony: its "patients" given a wide berth by all who sailed the straits. And in that same period, Emily Carr, that eccentric woman on Simcoe Street who saw what others didn't. She penetrated dark shores and forests with her paintbrush, and then dared to bring them back to the city on her canvasses.

Like Cadborosaurus, the sea serpent, until three decades ago, frequently spotted in these sun-jewelled waters. The thing described bore an uncanny resemblance to the west coast's *Huyitliik*, who "moves by wiggling back and forth," seen just sometimes by the first people, northeast of Tofino near Hot Springs Cove. Seen not at all, apparently, since powerboats started coming around.

These days in Eden, only bumps and ripples, ducks, ravens, sea lions, and a few killer whales are being reported.

Opposite: B.C. Ferries weave between Gulf Islands to Vancouver.

V a n c o u v e r   I s l a n d

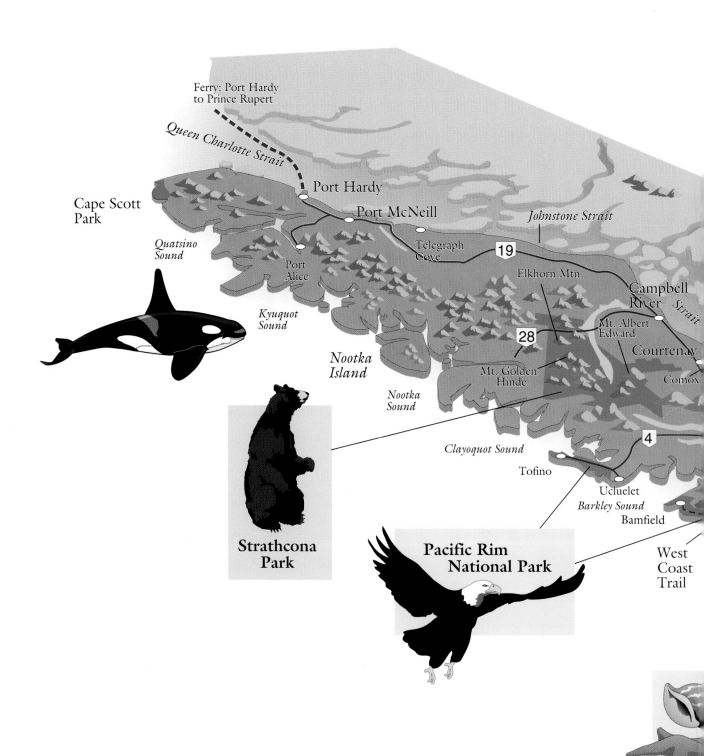

Ferry: Port Hardy
to Prince Rupert

Queen Charlotte Strait

Port Hardy

Cape Scott
Park

Port McNeill

Johnstone Strait

*Quatsino
Sound*

Telegraph
Cove

`19`

Elkhorn Mtn

Campbell
River

Strait

Port
Alice

*Kyuquot
Sound*

Mt. Albert
Edward

`28`

Courtenay

*Nootka
Island*

Mt. Golden
Hinde

Comox

*Nootka
Sound*

`4`

Clayoquot Sound

Tofino

Ucluelet

Barkley Sound

Bamfield

**Strathcona
Park**

**Pacific Rim
National Park**

West
Coast
Trail

Illustration by Rob Struthers

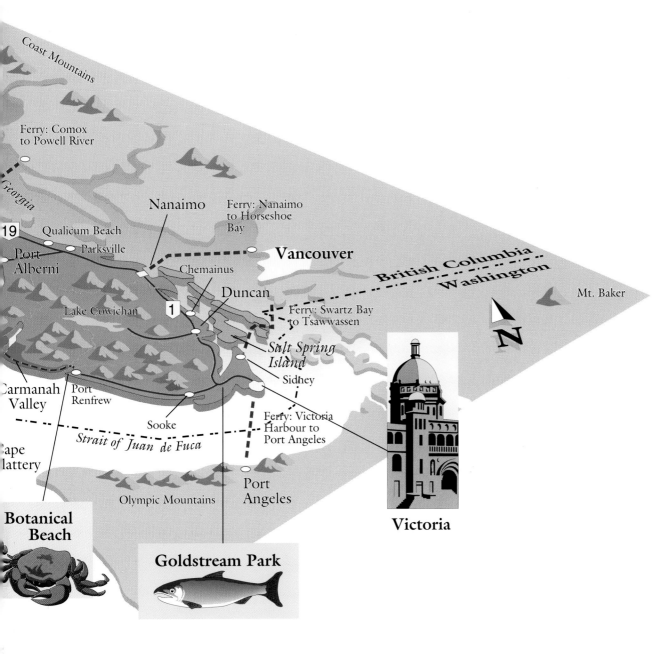

Coast Mountains

Ferry: Comox
to Powell River

Georgia

Nanaimo

Ferry: Nanaimo
to Horseshoe
Bay

19

Qualicum Beach

Parksville

Port
Alberni

Chemainus

Vancouver

British Columbia

Washington

Mt. Baker

Duncan

Lake Cowichan

1

Ferry: Swartz Bay
to Tsawwassen

Salt Spring
Island

Sidney

N

Carmanah
Valley

Port
Renfrew

Sooke

Ferry: Victoria
Harbour to
Port Angeles

Cape
Flattery

Strait of Juan de Fuca

Botanical
Beach

Olympic Mountains

Port
Angeles

Victoria

Goldstream Park